We Need To *Pray*

The key to unlocking your blessings and changing every situation is prayer

BARBARA GREEN

We Need To Pray

The key to unlocking your blessings and changing every situation is prayer

BARBARA GREEN

Printed in the United States of America by
T&J Publishers (Atlanta, GA.)
www.TandJPublishers.com

© Copyright 2018 by Barbara Green

All rights reserved. This book or parts thereof may not be reproduced in any form, stored in a retrieval system, or transmitted in any form by any means-electronic, mechanical, photocopy, recording, or otherwise-without prior written permission of the author, except as provided by United States of America copyright law.

ISBN: 978-0-9997806-9-5

To contact author, go to:
www.BGPrayerBook.com
trustgod7424@yahoo.com
Facebook: Barbara Green

ACKNOWLEDGMENTS

First I would like to thank God the Father, the Son and the Holy Spirit for allowing me to write this Prayer book through the unction of the Holy Spirit. Truly, God is faithful and without Him this prayer book would not have been possible.

I would like to thank my husband, Louis, our three sons Vandale, Ortagus, and Terrence who always support me in whatever God does in my life. I am forever grateful.

I thank my mother Mrs. Callener for being with me every step of the way. She always told me to pray because prayer works. Forever thankful for her. I thank my siblings, Mary, Nathaniel, and Joe. My siblings and I works close together in ministry and they are so encouraging in every way.

I would like to thank my Spiritual Father Bishop C.L. Carter, Sr. and First Lady Deborah V. Carter for all the knowledge, wisdom, prayers they have poured into my life. I would like to thank Pastor Gerry T. Anderson and First Lady Vanessa Anderson for all the support.

Lastly, I appreciate all my friends and families for pushing me to my destiny for the glory of God. Thanks to Pastor Victoria Burse, Prophet Nicole Henderson for helping me birth this book in Jesus name. Rev. Timothy Flemming Jr. I would like to thank you for all the hard work, and for blessing me to fulfill my purpose in Jesus name.

To God be the Glory!

"To be a Christian without prayer is no more possible than to be alive without breathing."
—*Martin Luther*

TABLE OF CONTENTS

Introduction	11
Chapter One: **The Communication Model of Prayer**	13
Chapter Two: **What Is Prayer?**	33
Chapter Three: **How To Pray Effectively**	39
Chapter Four: **Preparation For Prayer**	47
Chapter Five: **The Lord's Prayer**	53
Chapter Six: **Hindrances To Prayer**	67
Chapter Seven: **Different Types of Prayers**	73
Spiritual Warfare Prayer	85
Frequently Asked Questions About Prayer	89
More Bible Verses On Prayer	93

Introduction

WE ARE LIVING IN A TIME WHERE WE HAVE TO PRAY like never before. God wants us to communicate with Him. He wants us to open up and share with Him our hearts and minds. The Word of God tells us that men should always pray and not faint. Could it be that the main reason most people are hopeless and feel like giving up is there's not enough prayer going forth? The more we pray, the stronger our prayer lives become. The less we pray, the weaker our prayer lives become. But we must pray; we must communicate with our Father because He wants to hear from His children even though He already knows what is going on. Still, He wants to talk to us. Talking to the Heavenly Father will establish within us greater confidence in His power to protect and provide for us, and in His plan for our lives. When you want to get to know a person, you must sit down and talk with them; that is how you will be able to discover how they think and feel. Well, the same goes for our relationship with the Father. He desires that we spend time with Him and get to know Him intimately. We must take the time out of our daily lives and pray; after all, prayer is what changes our situations, circumstances, and people.

> The more we pray, the stronger our prayer lives become.

Trust me when I tell you, prayer won't just strengthen your bond with God, but it will benefit you in other ways. For example, prayer has been proven to relieve stress and anxiety. Jesus told us in Matthew 7:7-8 that by spending time in prayer, we release tension, worry, and uneasiness. Prayer does so much for us mentally, physically, and spiritually.

So many people are filled with anxiety in the world today. People are worried about so many things such as terrorism, death, financial trouble, family members, etc. But let me encourage you today to quit worrying and stressing over things, especially those things that are beyond your control, and start taking advantage of the privilege to speak with the Creator of the universe. It is He who holds all power in His hands to change things. Take your burdens and concerns to God in prayer. Ask God for what you need. Ask Him to protect and guide you. Remember what Jesus told us: If we keep on asking, and we will receive what we ask for; if we keep on seeking, we will find God; if we keep on knocking, the door will be opened unto us. Through prayer, we discern the will and mind of God concerning us.

CHAPTER 1
The Communication Model of Prayer

WHEN SEEKING TO UNDERSTAND PRAYER, IT WOULD behoove us to explore the Basic Model of Social Communication. This model of social communication is based on the communication model common in the field of information and communication technologies (ICT). This model has proved so useful that social psychologists "took it to mercy" and up to today, it is often used as a starting model. The Model understands communication as a linear activity as follows:

1. Sender (somehow) encodes the idea
2. The idea takes the form of a message (spoken, written, non-verbal, graphic ...)

3. Recipient decodes the message and (somehow) understands it
4. Subsequently, recipient provides feedback to the sender, whether he understood or misunderstood the message
5. Unfortunately, both the sender, the message (transmission) and the recipient are exposed to noise that blurs more or less the message[1]

As we relate the Basic Communication Model to prayer, we discern that the sender can be man or God (e.g., We pray to God, but we must also listen for God's answer.). The message is prayer and is said in a manner to be understood by the sender. However, even when we do not know what to pray for, the Holy Spirit intercedes on our behalf. God or man can be the recipient. God hears the prayer and man hears God's answer (i.e., feedback). We are reminded that throughout the entire process there is noise that try to hinder our prayers. Those noises can come in the form of distractions (e.g., sounds, body language, etc.), naysayers (e.g., "haters"), and Satan (who tries to make us doubt God and the power of prayer).

With this prelude, the following are the kings' prayers (underlined), God's hearing (in bold italics), His answers, and the results of those answered prayers (in bold).

The Prayer of King Hezekiah (2 Kings 20, KJV)

1 In those days was Hezekiah sick unto death. And the prophet Isaiah the son of Amoz came to him, and said

The Communication Model of Prayer

unto him, Thus saith the Lord, Set thine house in order; for thou shalt die, and not live.

<u>2 Then he turned his face to the wall, and prayed unto the Lord, saying,</u>

<u>3 I beseech thee, O Lord, remember now how I have walked before thee in truth and with a perfect heart, and have done that which is good in thy sight. And Hezekiah wept sore.</u>

4 And it came to pass, afore Isaiah was gone out into the middle court, that the word of the Lord came to him, saying,

5 Turn again, and tell Hezekiah the captain of my people, Thus saith the Lord, the God of David thy father, I have heard thy prayer, I have seen thy tears: behold, I will heal thee: on the third day thou shalt go up unto the house of the Lord.

6 And I will add unto thy days fifteen years; and I will deliver thee and this city out of the hand of the king of Assyria; and I will defend this city for mine own sake, and for my servant David's sake.

7 And Isaiah said, Take a lump of figs. And they took and laid it on the boil, and he recovered.

8 And Hezekiah said unto Isaiah, What shall be the sign that the Lord will heal me, and that I shall go up into the house of the Lord the third day?

9 And Isaiah said, This sign shalt thou have of the Lord, that the Lord will do the thing that he hath spoken: shall the shadow go forward ten degrees, or go back ten de-

grees?

10 And Hezekiah answered, It is a light thing for the shadow to go down ten degrees: nay, but let the shadow return backward ten degrees.

11 And Isaiah the prophet cried unto the Lord: and he brought the shadow ten degrees backward, by which it had gone down in the dial of Ahaz.

The Prayer of King David (1 Samuel 30, KJV)
(Notice the simple questions, profound answer, and astronomical result)

1 And it came to pass, when David and his men were come to Ziklag on the third day, that the Amalekites had invaded the south, and Ziklag, and smitten Ziklag, and burned it with fire;

2 And had taken the women captives, that were therein: they slew not any, either great or small, but carried them away, and went on their way.

3 So David and his men came to the city, and, behold, it was burned with fire; and their wives, and their sons, and their daughters, were taken captives.

4 Then David and the people that were with him lifted up their voice and wept, until they had no more power to weep.

5 And David's two wives were taken captives, Ahinoam the Jezreelitess, and Abigail the wife of Nabal the Carmelite.

The Communication Model of Prayer

6 And David was greatly distressed; for the people spake of stoning him, because the soul of all the people was grieved, every man for his sons and for his daughters: but David encouraged himself in the Lord his God.

7 And David said to Abiathar the priest, Ahimelech's son, I pray thee, bring me hither the ephod. And Abiathar brought thither the ephod to David.

<u>8 And David inquired at the Lord, saying, Shall I pursue after this troop? Shall I overtake them?</u> *And he answered him, Pursue: for thou shalt surely overtake them, and without fail recover all.*

9 So David went, he and the six hundred men that were with him, and came to the brook Besor, where those that were left behind stayed.

10 But David pursued, he and four hundred men: for two hundred abode behind, which were so faint that they could not go over the brook Besor.

11 And they found an Egyptian in the field, and brought him to David, and gave him bread, and he did eat; and they made him drink water;

12 And they gave him a piece of a cake of figs, and two clusters of raisins: and when he had eaten, his spirit came again to him: for he had eaten no bread, nor drunk any water, three days and three nights.

13 And David said unto him, To whom belongest thou? and whence art thou? And he said, I am a young man of Egypt, servant to an Amalekite; and my master left me, because three days agone I fell sick.

14 We made an invasion upon the south of the Cherethites, and upon the coast which belongeth to Judah, and upon the south of Caleb; and we burned Ziklag with fire.
15 And David said to him, Canst thou bring me down to this company? And he said, Swear unto me by God, that thou wilt neither kill me, nor deliver me into the hands of my master, and I will bring thee down to this company.
16 And when he had brought him down, behold, they were spread abroad upon all the earth, eating and drinking, and dancing, because of all the great spoil that they had taken out of the land of the Philistines, and out of the land of Judah.
17 And David smote them from the twilight even unto the evening of the next day: and there escaped not a man of them, save four hundred young men, which rode upon camels, and fled.
18 And David recovered all that the Amalekites had carried away: and David rescued his two wives.
19 And there was nothing lacking to them, neither small nor great, neither sons nor daughters, neither spoil, nor any thing that they had taken to them: **David recovered all.**

The Prayer of King Solomon (2 Chronicles 6, KJV)
1 Then said Solomon, The Lord hath said that he would dwell in the thick darkness.
2 But I have built an house of habitation for thee, and a place for thy dwelling forever.

The Communication Model of Prayer

3 And the king turned his face, and blessed the whole congregation of Israel: and all the congregation of Israel stood.

4 And he said, Blessed be the Lord God of Israel, who hath with his hands fulfilled that which he spake with his mouth to my father David, saying,

5 Since the day that I brought forth my people out of the land of Egypt I chose no city among all the tribes of Israel to build an house in, that my name might be there; neither chose I any man to be a ruler over my people Israel:

6 But I have chosen Jerusalem, that my name might be there; and have chosen David to be over my people Israel.

7 Now it was in the heart of David my father to build an house for the name of the Lord God of Israel.

8 But the Lord said to David my father, Forasmuch as it was in thine heart to build an house for my name, thou didst well in that it was in thine heart:

9 Notwithstanding thou shalt not build the house; but thy son which shall come forth out of thy loins, he shall build the house for my name.

10 The Lord therefore hath performed his word that he hath spoken: for I am risen up in the room of David my father, and am set on the throne of Israel, as the Lord promised, and have built the house for the name of the Lord God of Israel.

11 And in it have I put the ark, wherein is the covenant of the Lord, that he made with the children of Israel.

12 And he stood before the altar of the Lord in the pres-

ence of all the congregation of Israel, and spread forth his hands:

13 For Solomon had made a brasen scaffold of five cubits long, and five cubits broad, and three cubits high, and had set it in the midst of the court: and upon it he stood, and kneeled down upon his knees before all the congregation of Israel, and spread forth his hands toward heaven.

14 And said, O Lord God of Israel, there is no God like thee in the heaven, nor in the earth; which keepest covenant, and shewest mercy unto thy servants, that walk before thee with all their hearts:

15 Thou which hast kept with thy servant David my father that which thou hast promised him; and spakest with thy mouth, and hast fulfilled it with thine hand, as it is this day.

16 Now therefore, O Lord God of Israel, keep with thy servant David my father that which thou hast promised him, saying, There shall not fail thee a man in my sight to sit upon the throne of Israel; yet so that thy children take heed to their way to walk in my law, as thou hast walked before me.

17 Now then, O Lord God of Israel, let thy word be verified, which thou hast spoken unto thy servant David.

18 But will God in very deed dwell with men on the earth? behold, heaven and the heaven of heavens cannot contain thee; how much less this house which I have built!

19 Have respect therefore to the prayer of thy servant, and to his supplication, O Lord my God, to hearken unto

The Communication Model of Prayer

the cry and the prayer which thy servant prayeth before thee:

20 That thine eyes may be open upon this house day and night, upon the place whereof thou hast said that thou wouldest put thy name there; to hearken unto the prayer which thy servant prayeth toward this place.

21 Hearken therefore unto the supplications of thy servant, and of thy people Israel, which they shall make toward this place: hear thou from thy dwelling place, even from heaven; and when thou hearest, forgive.

22 If a man sin against his neighbour, and an oath be laid upon him to make him swear, and the oath come before thine altar in this house;

23 Then hear thou from heaven, and do, and judge thy servants, by requiting the wicked, by recompensing his way upon his own head; and by justifying the righteous, by giving him according to his righteousness.

24 And if thy people Israel be put to the worse before the enemy, because they have sinned against thee; and shall return and confess thy name, and pray and make supplication before thee in this house;

25 Then hear thou from the heavens, and forgive the sin of thy people Israel, and bring them again unto the land which thou gavest to them and to their fathers.

26 When the heaven is shut up, and there is no rain, because they have sinned against thee; yet if they pray toward this place, and confess thy name, and turn from their sin, when thou dost afflict them;

27 Then hear thou from heaven, and forgive the sin of thy servants, and of thy people Israel, when thou hast taught them the good way, wherein they should walk; and send rain upon thy land, which thou hast given unto thy people for an inheritance.

28 If there be dearth in the land, if there be pestilence, if there be blasting, or mildew, locusts, or caterpillars; if their enemies besiege them in the cities of their land; whatsoever sore or whatsoever sickness there be:

29 Then what prayer or what supplication soever shall be made of any man, or of all thy people Israel, when every one shall know his own sore and his own grief, and shall spread forth his hands in this house:

30 Then hear thou from heaven thy dwelling place, and forgive, and render unto every man according unto all his ways, whose heart thou knowest; (for thou only knowest the hearts of the children of men:)

31 That they may fear thee, to walk in thy ways, so long as they live in the land which thou gavest unto our fathers.

32 Moreover concerning the stranger, which is not of thy people Israel, but is come from a far country for thy great name's sake, and thy mighty hand, and thy stretched out arm; if they come and pray in this house;

33 Then hear thou from the heavens, even from thy dwelling place, and do according to all that the stranger calleth to thee for; that all people of the earth may know thy name, and fear thee, as doth thy people Israel, and may know that this house which I have built is called by

The Communication Model of Prayer

thy name.

34 If thy people go out to war against their enemies by the way that thou shalt send them, and they pray unto thee toward this city which thou hast chosen, and the house which I have built for thy name;

35 Then hear thou from the heavens their prayer and their supplication, and maintain their cause.

36 If they sin against thee, (for there is no man which sinneth not,) and thou be angry with them, and deliver them over before their enemies, and they carry them away captives unto a land far off or near;

37 Yet if they bethink themselves in the land whither they are carried captive, and turn and pray unto thee in the land of their captivity, saying, We have sinned, we have done amiss, and have dealt wickedly;

38 If they return to thee with all their heart and with all their soul in the land of their captivity, whither they have carried them captives, and pray toward their land, which thou gavest unto their fathers, and toward the city which thou hast chosen, and toward the house which I have built for thy name:

39 Then hear thou from the heavens, even from thy dwelling place, their prayer and their supplications, and maintain their cause, and forgive thy people which have sinned against thee.

40 Now, my God, let, I beseech thee, thine eyes be open, and let thine ears be attend unto the prayer that is made in this place.

<u>41 Now therefore arise, O Lord God, into thy resting place, thou, and the ark of thy strength: let thy priests, O Lord God, be clothed with salvation, and let thy saints rejoice in goodness.</u>
<u>42 O Lord God, turn not away the face of thine anointed: remember the mercies of David thy servant.</u>

God's Answer to Solomon's Prayer (2 Chronicles 7, KJV)

1 Now when Solomon had made an end of praying, the fire came down from heaven, and consumed the burnt offering and the sacrifices; and the glory of the Lord filled the house.

2 And the priests could not enter into the house of the Lord, because the glory of the Lord had filled the Lord's house.

3 And when all the children of Israel saw how the fire came down, and the glory of the Lord upon the house, they bowed themselves with their faces to the ground upon the pavement, and worshipped, and praised the Lord, saying, For he is good; for his mercy endureth forever.

4 Then the king and all the people offered sacrifices before the Lord.

5 And king Solomon offered a sacrifice of twenty and two thousand oxen, and an hundred and twenty thousand sheep: so the king and all the people dedicated the house of God.

6 And the priests waited on their offices: the Levites also

The Communication Model of Prayer

with instruments of music of the Lord, which David the king had made to praise the Lord, because his mercy endureth for ever, when David praised by their ministry; and the priests sounded trumpets before them, and all Israel stood.

7 Moreover Solomon hallowed the middle of the court that was before the house of the Lord: for there he offered burnt offerings, and the fat of the peace offerings, because the brasen altar which Solomon had made was not able to receive the burnt offerings, and the meat offerings, and the fat.

8 Also at the same time Solomon kept the feast seven days, and all Israel with him, a very great congregation, from the entering in of Hamath unto the river of Egypt.

9 And in the eighth day they made a solemn assembly: for they kept the dedication of the altar seven days, and the feast seven days.

10 And on the three and twentieth day of the seventh month he sent the people away into their tents, glad and merry in heart for the goodness that the Lord had shewed unto David, and to Solomon, and to Israel his people.

11 Thus Solomon finished the house of the Lord, and the king's house: and all that came into Solomon's heart to make in the house of the Lord, and in his own house, he prosperously effected.

12 And the Lord appeared to Solomon by night, and said unto him, I have heard thy prayer, and have chosen this place to myself for an house of sacrifice.

13 If I shut up heaven that there be no rain, or if I command the locusts to devour the land, or if I send pestilence among my people;

14 If my people, which are called by my name, shall humble themselves, and pray, and seek my face, and turn from their wicked ways; then will I hear from heaven, and will forgive their sin, and will heal their land.

15 Now mine eyes shall be open, and mine ears attent unto the prayer that is made in this place.

16 For now have I chosen and sanctified this house, that my name may be there forever: and mine eyes and mine heart shall be there perpetually.

17 And as for thee, if thou wilt walk before me, as David thy father walked, and do according to all that I have commanded thee, and shalt observe my statutes and my judgments;

18 Then will I establish the throne of thy kingdom, according as I have covenanted with David thy father, saying, There shall not fail thee a man to be ruler in Israel.

19 But if ye turn away, and forsake my statutes and my commandments, which I have set before you, and shall go and serve other gods, and worship them;

20 Then will I pluck them up by the roots out of my land which I have given them; and this house, which I have sanctified for my name, will I cast out of my sight, and will make it to be a proverb and a byword among all nations.

21 And this house, which is high, shall be an astonishment to every one that passeth by it; so that he shall say, Why hath the Lord done thus unto this land, and unto this house?

22 And it shall be answered, Because they forsook the Lord God of their fathers, which brought them forth out of the land of Egypt, and laid hold on other gods, and worshipped them, and served them: therefore hath he brought all this evil upon them.

THE PRAYER OF KING JEHOSHAPHAT (2 CHRONICLES CHAPTER 20, KJV)

1 It came to pass after this also, that the children of Moab, and the children of Ammon, and with them other beside the Ammonites, came against Jehoshaphat to battle."

2 Then there came some that told Jehoshaphat, saying, There cometh a great multitude against thee from beyond the sea on this side Syria; and, behold, they be in Hazazontamar, which is Engedi.

3 And Jehoshaphat feared, and set himself to seek the Lord, and proclaimed a fast throughout all Judah.

4 And Judah gathered themselves together, to ask help of the Lord: even out of all the cities of Judah they came to seek the Lord.

5 And Jehoshaphat stood in the congregation of Judah and Jerusalem, in the house of the Lord, before the new court,

6 And said, O Lord God of our fathers, art not thou God in heaven? And rulest not thou over all the kingdoms of the heathen? And in thine hand is there not power and might, so that none is able to withstand thee?

7 Art not thou our God, who didst drive out the inhabitants of this land before thy people Israel, and gavest it to the seed of Abraham thy friend forever?

8 And they dwelt therein, and have built thee a sanctuary therein for thy name, saying,

9 If, when evil cometh upon us, as the sword, judgment, or pestilence, or famine, we stand before this house, and in thy presence, (for thy name is in this house,) and cry unto thee in our affliction, then thou wilt hear and help.

10 And now, behold, the children of Ammon and Moab and mount Seir, whom thou wouldest not let Israel invade, when they came out of the land of Egypt, but they turned from them, and destroyed them not;

11 Behold, I say, how they reward us, to come to cast us out of thy possession, which thou hast given us to inherit.

12 O our God, wilt thou not judge them? For we have no might against this great company that cometh against us; neither know we what to do: but our eyes are upon thee.

13 And all Judah stood before the Lord, with their little ones, their wives, and their children.

14 Then upon Jahaziel the son of Zechariah, the son of Benaiah, the son of Jeiel, the son of Mattaniah, a Levite of the sons of Asaph, came the Spirit of the Lord in the midst of the congregation;

The Communication Model of Prayer

15 And he said, Hearken ye, all Judah, and ye inhabitants of Jerusalem, and thou king Jehoshaphat, Thus saith the Lord unto you, Be not afraid nor dismayed by reason of this great multitude; for the battle is not yours, but God's.

16 Tomorrow go ye down against them: behold, they come up by the cliff of Ziz; and ye shall find them at the end of the brook, before the wilderness of Jeruel.

17 Ye shall not need to fight in this battle: set yourselves, stand ye still, and see the salvation of the Lord with you, O Judah and Jerusalem: fear not, nor be dismayed; tomorrow go out against them: for the Lord will be with you.

18 And Jehoshaphat bowed his head with his face to the ground: and all Judah and the inhabitants of Jerusalem fell before the Lord, worshipping the Lord.

19 And the Levites, of the children of the Kohathites, and of the children of the Korhites, stood up to praise the Lord God of Israel with a loud voice on high.

20 And they rose early in the morning, and went forth into the wilderness of Tekoa: and as they went forth, Jehoshaphat stood and said, Hear me, O Judah, and ye inhabitants of Jerusalem; believe in the Lord your God, so shall ye be established; believe his prophets, so shall ye prosper.

21 And when he had consulted with the people, he appointed singers unto the Lord, and that should praise the beauty of holiness, as they went out before the army, and

to say, Praise the Lord; for his mercy endureth forever.

22 And when they began to sing and to praise, the Lord set ambushments against the children of Ammon, Moab, and mount Seir, which were come against Judah; and they were smitten.

23 For the children of Ammon and Moab stood up against the inhabitants of mount Seir, utterly to slay and destroy them: and when they had made an end of the inhabitants of Seir, every one helped to destroy another.

24 And when Judah came toward the watch tower in the wilderness, they looked unto the multitude, and, behold, they were dead bodies fallen to the earth, and none escaped.

25 And when Jehoshaphat and his people came to take away the spoil of them, they found among them in abundance both riches with the dead bodies, and precious jewels, which they stripped off for themselves, more than they could carry away: and they were three days in gathering of the spoil, it was so much.

26 And on the fourth day they assembled themselves in the valley of Berachah; for there they blessed the Lord: therefore the name of the same place was called, The valley of Berachah, unto this day.

The Communication Model of Prayer

We Need To Pray

CHAPTER 2
What Is Prayer?

According to the Student Bible Dictionary Expanded and Updated Edition, prayer is talking and listening to God; an intimate fellowship with God (1Kings 8:20; Matthew 21:22). Prayer is defined as "a spiritual communion with God or an object or worship, as in supplication, thanksgiving, adoration, or confession" (www.Dictionary.com). And since God is invisible, it requires faith to communicate with Him, which means you must believe He's there even though you can't see Him. Prayer is also the basis for developing a relationship with God (Psalm 66:18; James 5:16). Elements of prayer include praising, thanking, confessing, asking, interceding (praying for others), and receiving.[1] When we find time to get away

> ...prayer is talking and listening to God; an intimate fellowship...

- go to someplace where there aren't many distractions, a place where we can be still and listen quietly - we'll begin to hear the Holy Spirit speaking back to us.

Prayer is the means by which we get to know God and His will for our lives. Prayer is our line of communication with God; it touches the heart of God. If we want to stay connected with God, prayer is the key. You know how it is when family and friends come together and spend time together: time spent together draws them closer. So, if spending time with families and friends creates a stronger bond, then what do you think happens when we spend time with God? It develops a stronger bond between us; it strengthens our relationship with God. One of the signs that you love someone is you'll want to spend time with them and communicate with them as often as you can. If we say we love God, then we should demonstrate it through our actions - we should do whatever it takes to set aside time for Him in prayer. God demonstrated His love for us by sending His Son Jesus to die on the cross for our sins; therefore, we should love Him enough to at least do the simplest thing: take some time to pray.

Prayer is communication between man and God, which means it is a two-way street: not only do we talk to God, but we allow God to talk to us. We must be willing to listen to Him as He speaks to us in various ways: through the Holy Spirit and through His Word. I have learned that when we communicate with God, there should come a point where we quiet down so that we can hear what God is saying

What Is Prayer?

to us. God is speaking, but are we listening. To listen simply means "to give ear to; to pay attention to sound; to hear something with thoughtful attention" (Merriam Webster). When you think of prayer, think of a child having a conversation with his or her father. It is natural for a child to ask his or her father for the things he or she needs. Don't make prayer a complicated thing, because it isn't; it simply communicating with the Creator of heaven and earth.

As we pray, we're entering into a dialogue with God. Such dialogue involves cries for help as revealed in Exodus 3:7, which reads: "And the Lord said, I have surely seen the affliction of my people which are in Egypt, and have heard their cry by reason of their taskmasters; for I know their sorrows; and I am come down to deliver them out of the hand of the Egyptians, and to bring them up out of that land unto a good land and a large, unto a land flowing with milk and honey; unto the place of the Canaanites, and the Hittites, and the Amorites, and the Perizzites, and the Hivites, and the Jebusites." Here, God is having a conversation with Moses about His people who were slaves in Egypt; He was sharing with Moses His plans. Notice that God desires to share with us His plans, what's in His heart, not just hear what's in ours. Prayer is a conversation about God's will according to Exodus 3:1-4:17.

> Prayer is the means by which we get to know God and His will for our lives. Prayer is our line of communication with God...

We Need To Pray

When we think about a dialogue, we understand that this not one person doing all of the talking; there is more than one person involved. Whenever two people are talking at the same time, no one will understand what the other person is saying. So we have to quiet down at some point and listen. God said in Psalm 46:10, "Be still and know that I am God. I will be exalted among the heathen, I will be exalted in the earth." Also, Jesus said in John 10:27, "My sheep hear my voice and I know them, and they follow me: and I give unto them eternal life, and they shall never perish, neither shall any man pluck them out of my hand." Through prayer, we get to know the voice of God; we begin to distinguish His voice from others and our own.

When we pray to God we must express our adoration of Him. Adoration is simply an "attitude of worship characterized by love and reverence towards God" (Bible Gateway). Just as you would express your love and adoration for someone you value and cherish, you should do the same for God. David was masterful at doing this (Psalm 31:23, Psalm 116:1).

Not only do we express our adoration for God when praying, but we maintain a strong sense of respect and worship for Him. Worshiping God is also key to establishing a relationship with Him as revealed in John 4:23-24:

> "But the hour cometh, and now is, when the true worshippers shall worship the Father in spirit and in truth; for the Father seeketh such to worship him.

What Is Prayer?

God is a Spirit: and they that worship him must worship him in spirit and in truth."

Prayer is also "beseeching the Lord" as revealed in Exodus 32:11; it is the act of "pouring out the soul before the Lord" according to 1 Samuel 1:15; it is "praying and crying to heaven" according to 2 Chronicles 32:20; it is "seeking unto God and making supplication" according to Job 8:5; it is "drawing near to God" according to Psalms 73:28; and it requires "bowing the knees" according to Ephesians 3:14 (Easton's Bible Dictionary).

> Through prayer, we get to know the voice of God; we begin to distinguish His voice from others and our own.

Jesus began His ministry with prayer and He ended it with prayer. Even while Jesus was on the cross, He was praying. At one point, He prayed, "Father, into your hands I commend my spirit" (Luke 23:46, NKJV). Here are more examples of Jesus praying:

Jesus prayed in crucial moments, including when it was time to choose His disciples. He made sure He prayed before aligning Himself with anyone as expressed in Mark 3:13, which says, "Jesus went up on a mountainside and called to him those he wanted, and they came to him."

Mark 9:2: "After six days Jesus took Peter, James, and John with him and led them up a high mountain, where they were all alone. There he was transfigured before them."

Luke 5:16: "And he withdrew himself into the wilderness, and prayed."

Matthew 26:36-39: "Then cometh Jesus with them unto a place called Gethsemane, and saith unto the disciples, Sit ye here, while I go and pray yonder. And he took with him Peter and the two sons of Zebedee, and began to be sorrowful and very heavy. Then saith he unto them, My soul is exceeding sorrowful, even unto death, tarry ye here and watch with me. And he went a little further, and fell on his face, and prayed, saying, O my Father, if it be possible, let this cup pass from me: nevertheless not as I will, but as thou wilt."

CHAPTER 3
How To Pray Effectively

THE WORD "EFFECTIVE" MEANS "SUCCESSFUL IN producing a desired or intended result; existing in fact, though not formally acknowledged as such" (English by Oxford Dictionaries). When we pray to the Heavenly Father, we should strive to pray effectively. Here is a list of how we can pray effectively:

1. We always want to pray in Jesus name. There is power in the name of Jesus according to John 14:13-14, which reads:

> John 14:13: "Whatsoever ye shall ask in my name, that will I do, that the Father may be glorified in the Son." John 14:14: "If ye shall ask anything in my name, I will do it."

Regarding the name of God, here are a few names given to us in the Bible:

- Jehovah-jireh (the Lord will provide - Genesis 22:14)
- Jehovah-nissi (the Lord my banner - Exodus 17:15)
- Jehovah-shalom (the Lord send peace - Judges 6:24)
- Jehovah-shammah (the Lord is there - Ezekiel 48:35)
- Jehovah-tsidkenu (the Lord our righteousness - Jeremiah 33:16)

Most importantly, it is important to know that there is power in the one name given to men by which we may be saved (Acts 4:12), which is the name of Jesus. Whenever we pray, we must always pray in the name of Jesus. Everything we need is in His name. In John 14:13, Jesus said, "And whatsoever ye shall ask in my name, that will I do, that the Father may be glorified in the Son. If ye shall ask any thing in my name, I will do it." When you pray, pray by faith and believe that God will perform His promises in our lives in Jesus name. There is no name above the name of Jesus. Philippians 2:9-11 says, "Wherefore God also hath highly exalted him, and given him a name which is above every name: That at the name of Jesus every knee should bow, of things in heaven, and things in earth, and things under the earth; And that every tongue should confess that Jesus Christ is Lord, to the glory of God the Father."

2. We must pray according to the will of God. There is a cri-

terion we must observe and follow as it pertains to effective prayer, and praying according to God's will and not ours is one of the most important requirements. When seeking to know God's will, it's important that we know that it is revealed to us through His Word. His word reveals to us how we should live as Believers. Psalm 143:10 says, "Teach me to do thy will; for thou art my God: thy spirit is good; lead me into the land of uprightness."

> Whenever we pray, we must always pray in the name of Jesus. Everything we need is in His name.

The Word of God reveals the will of God for our lives; therefore, it is essential that we pray according to the Word. God's Word will change our lives. Here are a few verses about the importance of the Word of God pertaining to prayer:

> John 1:1: "In the beginning was the Word, and the Word was with God, and the Word was God."
> Matthew 4:1-4: "Then was Jesus led up of the Spirit into the wilderness to be tempted of the devil. And when he had fasted forty days and forty nights, he was af-terward a hungered. And when the tempter came to him, he said, If thou be the Son of God, command that these stones be made bread. But he answered and said, It is written Man shall not live by bread alone, but by every word that proceedeth out of the mouth of God."

Isaiah 40:8: "The grass withereth, the flower fadeth: but the word of our God shall stand for ever." Mark 13:31: "Heaven and earth shall pass away: but my words shall not pass away."

If you don't know the will of God for your life, ask God to teach you His will. This is what David did in Psalm 143:10. He prayed, "Teach me to do thy will; for thou art my God: thy spirit is good; lead me into the hand of uprightness." Again, this is one of the privileges of prayer. We are able to go directly to the source of all creation Himself and receive guidance regarding His will for our lives as revealed in Psalm 25:4: "Show me thy ways, O Lord; teach me thy paths. Lead me in thy truth, and teach me: for thou art the God of my salvation; on thee do I wait all the day." When you are praying for God's will, ask Him to lead you in His truth because He is the only one who can lead us in the right path (the path of righteousness).

There also comes a time when you have to wait on the Lord, and this is the part that seems a little difficult, but God said wait on:

Psalm 27:14: "Wait on the Lord: be of good courage, and he shall strengthen thine heart: wait, I say, on the Lord."

Psalm 37:9: "For evildoers shall be cut off: but those that wait upon the Lord, they shall inherit the earth."

Isaiah 40:30-31: "Even the youths shall faint and be weary, and the young men shall utterly fall: But they that wait upon the Lord shall renew their strength; they shall mount up with wings as eagles; they shall run, and not be weary; and they shall walk, and not faint."

Jesus was about the Heavenly Father's business. It is important that we learn to follow after Jesus' example so that like Him, we will learn to do the will of the Father. That's what Jesus desires of us as revealed in John 4:34, which says, "Jesus saith unto them, My meat is to do the will of him that sent me, and to finish his work."

> If you don't know the will of God for your life, ask God to teach you His will.

Jesus was focused on doing the will of God the Father in the earth. David prophesied about Christ in Psalm 40:7-9 when he wrote, "Then said I, Lo, I come: in the volume of the book it is written of me. I delight to do thy will, O my God: yea, thy law is within my heart."

3. We must have a sincere and true faith. What is faith? It is defined as "A belief, trust, and loyalty to a person or thing" by the Baker's Evangelical Dictionary of Biblical Theology. The Bible Gateway New Century version defines faith this way: "Faith means being sure of the things we hope for and knowing that something is real even if we do not see it" (Hebrews

11:1). The Word of God tells us in Mark 11:24, "Therefore I say unto you, What things soever ye desire, when ye pray, believe that ye receive them, and ye shall have them. Without faith its impossible to please God." Here are a few more verses that talk about the importance of having faith while praying:

> Hebrews 11:6 says, "But without faith it is impossible to please him: for he that cometh to God must believe that he is, and that he is a rewarder of them that diligently seek him." (We must believe that God will reward us when we diligently or sincerely seek after Him.)
> 1 Chronicles 16:11: "Seek the Lord and his strength, seek his face continually."
> Isaiah 55:6 "Seek ye the Lord while he may be found, call ye upon him while he is near."

There's a reward for seeking the Lord as revealed in 2 Chronicles 26:5, which says, "And he sought God in the days of Zechariah, who had understanding in the visions of God: and as long as he sought the Lord, God made him to prosper."

4. We must put action behind our words. The Bible explains the importance of not only having faith, but also having works. James 2:17-20 says,

> 17 "Even so faith, if it hath not works, is dead, being

alone.

18 "Yea, a man may say, Thou hast faith, and I have works: shew me thy faith without thy works, and I will shew thee my faith by my works.

19 "Thou believest that there is one God; thou does well: the devils also believe, and tremble.

20 "But wilt thou know, O vain man, that faith without works is dead?"

5. Stand fast in the faith. The Bible tells us in Hebrews 10:23, "Let us hold fast the profession of our faith without wavering; for he is faithful that promised." Keep in mind that God rewards us for having faith in Him; He rewards our faith when we pray. This is what the Bible says about the reward we receive for having faith:

Matthew 17:20: "And Jesus said unto them, Because of your unbelief: for verily I say unto you, If ye have faith as a grain of mustard seed, ye shall say unto this mountain, Remove hence to yonder place; and it shall remove; and nothing shall be impossible unto you."

6. We must forgive while praying. Here's what the Bible says about forgiving others:

Luke 17:3-4: "Take heed to yourselves: If thy brother trespass against thee, rebuke him; and if he repent, forgive him; and if he trespass against thee seven

times in a day, and seven times in a day turn again to thee, saying, I repent; thou shalt forgive him."
Ephesians 4:32: "And be ye kind one to another, tenderhearted, forgiving one another, even as God for Christ's sake hath forgiven you."

7. We must practice obedience to God while praying. The Bible says in Isaiah 1:19-20, "If ye be willing and obedient, ye shall eat the good of the land: but if ye refuse and rebel, ye shall be devoured with the sword; for the mouth of the Lord hath spoken it." Also, Deuteronomy 7:9 says, "Know therefore that the Lord thy God, he is God, the faithful God, which keepeth covenant and mercy with them that love him and keep his commandments to a thousand generations."

(Note: This material came out of What does the Bible say about..,. The Ultimate Answer Book by Brian Ridolfi; Published by AMG Publishers 6815 Shallowford Rd. Chattanooga, Tn. 37421)

CHAPTER 4
Preparation For Prayer

The word "prepare" means "to get ready for something" (Vocabulary.com). There are so many things we often prepare for in life: weddings, vacations, birthdays, etc. Likewise, it is important that we realize that we must prepare for prayer. When we go to our Father in prayer we can't go to Him any kind of way. Oftentimes, our hearts and mind are not prepared to enter into prayer because there are too many things preoccupying our minds causing our attention to be scattered in so many directions. When preparing to pray, it is important that we do the following:

1. We need to confess our sins. Truthfully, we all have sins to confess. We all have areas in our lives that we need God to help us in. Here are a couple of Bible verses that explain to

us the importance of confessing our sins before asking God for anything else:

> 1 John 1:9: "If we confess our sins, he is faithful and just to forgive us our sins, and to cleanse us from all unrighteousness."
>
> Psalms 32:5: "I acknowledged my sin unto thee, and mine iniquity have I not hid. I said, I will confess my transgressions unto the Lord; and thou forgivest the iniquity of my sin. Selah."

Our Father cannot lie. Numbers 23:19 says, "God is not a man, that he should lie; neither the son of man, that he should repent: hath he said, and shall he not do it? Or hath he spoken, and shall he not make it good?" God is the one who is faithful and not only faithful but he is just to forgive us our sins:

> ...it is important that we realize that we must prepare for prayer. When we go to our Father in prayer we can't go to Him any kind of way.

> "For all have sinned, and come short of the glory of God; Being justified freely by his grace through the redemption that is in Christ Jesus." (Romans 3:23-24)

The word "justified" in the Greek is *dikaioe* and it means "to be acquitted, declared 'Not guilty' in a judicial sense; to be

Preparation For Prayer

declared righteous in God's sight" (Life in the Spirit Study Bible). The word "redemption" means "the action of saving or being saved from sin, error, or evil; the action of regaining or gaining possession of something in exchange for payment, or clearing a debt" (English Oxford Living Dictionaries). It is a blessing to be redeemed by Jesus Christ who paid the price for our sins over two-thousand years ago.

2. The next step we must take in the prayer process is repent. The word "repentance" means "A feeling of regret; a changing of the mind, or a turning from sin to God." With regards to the concept of regret, even God experiences this emotion as revealed in Joel 2:13, Jonah 4:2, and Genesis 6:6-7, which tells us that God was sorry (regretful) that He had created the human race.[1]

Here are a few Bible verses that speak about repentance:

> Matthew 3:1-2: "In those days came John the Baptist, preaching in the wilderness of Judea, and saying, Repent ye: for the kingdom of heaven is at hand."
> 2 Chronicles 7:14 (NIV): "If my people, who are called by my name, will humble themselves and pray and seek my face and turn from their wicked ways, then I will hear from heaven, and I will forgive their sin and will heal their land."

God loves us all and desires that we repent and turn away

from sin. Why? It's because He is such a caring and compassionate God. As 2 Peter 3:9 reveals, "God is not slack concerning His promise, as some men count slackness, but is longsuffering toward us, not willing that any should perish, but that all should come to repentance" (NIV).

3. We must ask God for forgiveness of our sins. There is no one on this earth who is perfect. We have all fallen short of the glory of God. When you go into prayer tell God whatever it is that is going on—He already know, but He just wants to hear from you. You don't have to go to God feeling ashamed or bad about the things you've done because He is loving and merciful; instead, all He wants is that you come to Him with a sincere heart. God already knows our hearts, so there is nothing that is hidden from Him. When you go to the Father ask Him to create in you "a clean heart, O God, and renew a right spirit within me" as David prayed in Psalm 51:10. After that, ask Him to "Search me O God, and know my heart: try me, and know my thoughts: And see if there is any wicked way in me, and lead me in the way everlasting." This is between you and God. Don't worry about anyone else's heart. Just make sure your heart is right with the Lord.

4. After you have confessed your sins, repented, and asked for forgiveness, now is the time for you to enter into God's presence, or as the Bible says in Psalm 100:4, "Enter into his gates with thanksgiving, and into his courts with praise, be thankful unto him and bless his name." When you enter into

that place of praise the whole atmosphere changes, even the spirit of heaviness leaves you. Psalm 145:1-3 says,

> "I will exalt you, my God the King; I will praise your name for ever and ever. Every day I will praise you and extol your name for ever and ever. Great is the Lord and most worthy of praise his greatness no one can fathom."

Praising God invites His presence into our lives. Psalm 16:11 says,

> "Thou wilt show me the path of life: in thy presence is fullness of joy; at thy right hand there are pleasures for evermore."

Joy and peace are just two of the incredible things we experience in God's presence, but the path into God's presence is spending time thanking Him while in worship. Enter into the Holy of Holies, which simply means we must draw near to the presence of God. It's an awesome feeling to experience the glorious presence of God. There's nothing else like it.

5. We must live in the Spirit of God (the Holy Spirit). We must ask the Holy Spirit in prayer to have His way in our lives and give Him permission to do whatever He wants to do while in prayer. Ask the Holy Spirit to lead, guide, and

direct your steps while communing with Him in prayer. Ask the Holy Spirit to help you to remain focused on God and His will for your life. Ask Him to remove all distractions and hindrances away from you that are blocking you from focusing on and doing God's will. Ask Him. He's listening. Talk to Him just like you would your best friend. He's real and He hears your prayers.

In conclusion, remember that we must prepare ourselves for prayer. We shouldn't go to God any kind of way, but go to Him with a heart of repentance. Always remember that God loves you and He loves hearing from you.

CHAPTER 5

The Lord's Prayer

THE LORD'S PRAYER IS THE MOST POPULAR PRAYER IN the Bible; it's the prayer we were most likely taught as children. This is the model prayer, the prayer Jesus instructed us to pray daily. In Matthew 6:1-13, we find Jesus teaching His followers about the importance of prayer while instructing them on how to pray. This is what He said,

> *1 Take heed that ye do not your alms before men, to be seen of them: otherwise ye have no reward of your Father which is in heaven.*
> *2 Therefore when thou doest thine alms, do not sound a trumpet before thee, as the hypocrites do in the synagogues and in the streets, that they may have glory of men. Verily I say unto you, They have their reward.*

Alms ("money, food, or other donations given to the poor or needy; anything given as charity") (www.Dictionary.com). The word "hypocrites" refer to people who do good acts for appearance only, not out of compassion or other good motives (Life Application Study Bible). Here, Jesus is letting us know that when you give to the needy, you should not announce it with trumpets like the hypocrites do to get attention. The hypocrites want to be praise by people, but God said they have their reward.

> *3 But when thou doest alms, let not thy left hand know what thy right hand doeth:*

Whenever you give to the needy, do not let your left hand know what your right hand is doing. In other words, we need to make sure our motives are right whenever we give. Are you giving to be recognized or to get something in return? Whenever you give to God and others, make sure your motives are pure.

> *4 That thine alms may be in secret: and thy Father which seeth in secret himself shall reward thee openly.*

When you give, do it quietly. You don't have to let everyone know what you are doing. You want to make sure that whatever you do for someone else your actions are God-centered and not self-centered. Romans 8:8 says, "Those controlled by the sinful nature cannot please God."

The Lord's Prayer

> 5 And when thou prayest, thou shalt not be as the hypocrites are: for they love to pray standing in the synagogues and in the corners of the streets, that they may be seen of men. Verily I say unto you, They have their reward.

These love not to pray, but to pray where they will be seen, and pray that they may be seen. So the Pharisees took pains to be in some public place, where they could strike an attitude of prayer in the sight of many observers. The same spirit is often seen still.[1]

> 6 But thou, when thou prayest, enter into thy closet, and when thou hast shut thy door, pray to thy Father which is in secret; and thy Father which seeth in secret shall reward thee openly.

The word "closet," as used in the New Testament, signifies properly a storehouse (Luke 12:24, and hence a place of privacy and retirement(Matthew 6:6;Luke 12:3) (Easton's Bible Dictionary). The Greek word for "closet" is *temian*, which means "an inner chamber or a secret room." You, as children of God, should have some place to be alone with God. Jesus often went away to pray. Matthew 14:23 says, "After He had sent the crowds away, He went up on the mountain by Himself to pray, and

> Whenever you give to God and others, make sure your motives are pure.

when it was evening, He was there alone." Also, Luke 6:12 says, "It was at this time that He went off to the mountain to pray, and He spent the whole night in prayer to God." There comes a time when you need to separate yourselves from all the things that are going on and spend time with the Lord. God longs for us to spend that quality time with Him. He wants us to communicate with Him. So you need to get quiet and listen to what God is saying to you. God is speaking, but are you listening? Sometimes you can be so busy with the things of this life that you miss out on what God is saying. He wants us to get alone and talk to Him and also listen to what He has to say in this hour.

> *7 But when ye pray, use not vain repetitions, as the heathen do: for they think that they shall be heard for their much speaking.*

The NIV translates the phrase "vain repetitions" as "keep on babbling." God doesn't want us to pray vain repetitions where there is no real substance. "Vain" means "having no real substance, value, or importance; empty; void; worthless; unsatisfying" (Webster's Revised Unabridged Dictionary). God want us to pray sincerely from the heart. Jesus took time to explain to His disciples that they should not pray like the heathens. A heathen is someone that lacks any knowledge of the true and living God (Jehovah); they worship idol gods, including themselves. Our sincerity, lifestyles, and obedience to God's Word give our prayers great meaning. Remember:

The Lord's Prayer

Prayer is a heart issue. This is why Jesus warned us not to imitate the lives, actions, and activities of the heathen. God is not going to answer a prayer because you say it repetitiously; He answers because you obey His Word.

Jesus continued in His explanation on how to pray effectively,

> 8 Be not ye therefore like unto them: for your Father knoweth what things ye have need of, before ye ask him.
> 9 After this manner therefore pray ye: Our Father which art in heaven, Hallowed be thy name.

There's a reason Jesus told us to refer to God the Father as "our Father." When we call God "Father" we make our relationship with Him personal. God no longer becomes "the man upstairs"; He becomes an intimate part of our daily lives. When we acknowledge God as our "Father who art in Heaven," we see ourselves in a different light: as children of God who have the right to present our hearts to Him as a child would their own father.

Galatians 4:6 tells us "And because ye are sons, God hath sent forth the Spirit of his Son into your hearts, crying, Abba, Father." We also acknowledge where our true home lies, remembering that this earth is not our home. Heaven is the place where we are headed if we have accepted Jesus as our personal Saviour according to Romans 10:9-10. It is the place where we belong.

We Need To Pray

Again, Jesus told us to start out by acknowledging God as "our" Father, which means He's not just my Father and your Father, but He is a Father to all of His creation. This doesn't mean everyone is in alignment with His will and is heaven-bound. God loves us all although He can't allow sin into His presence. Furthermore, it is important that we know there is only one name we must pray in when praying, and that is the name of Jesus, which is the only name given to men whereby we may be saved according to Acts 4:12. Our authority in prayer only comes when we pray in the name of Jesus. It is before that name that every knee shall bow and every tongue should confess.

Jesus taught us in this prayer how to properly address God. Knowing how to address God now, why would we misaddress Him or call Him by any other name? This is the formula for successful prayer. Using this formula, we have been granted access to the throne room of God; we've been allowed to enter boldly before God's Throne of Grace! We must thank Jesus for making this possible. It is because of Jesus that we can have an intimate relationship with God and be able to call Him Father. That's what God desires from us anyway - to call Him "Father" as revealed in the Word:

> Malachi 2:10 (KJV): "Have we not all one father? Hath not one God created us? Why do we deal treacherously every man against his brother, by profaning the covenant of our fathers?"
> Galatians 4:6 (KJV): "And because ye are sons, God

hath sent forth the Spirit of his Son into your hearts, crying, Abba, Father."
Psalm 103:19 (KJV): "The Lord hath prepared his throne in the heavens; and his kingdom ruleth over all. God's name is holy. His name is sanctified."

Let's continue with Jesus' prayer. The next thing Jesus tells us to say in prayer is,

10 "Thy kingdom come…"

The word "kingdom" means "the rank, quality, state, or attributes of a king; royal authority; sovereign power; rule; dominion; monarchy" (Webster's Revised Unabridged Dictionary). The kingdom of God (or heaven) carries the idea of God coming into the world to assert His power, glory, and rights against Satan's dominion and the present course of this world. It is more than salvation or the church; it is God expressing Himself powerfully in all His works (Life in the Spirit Study Bible).

The Kingdom of God refers to the coming rule and reign of God through Christ on the earth during Christ's second coming. Also, the Apostle Paul explains further about the Kingdom of God in Romans 14:17 where he writes, "For the kingdom of God is not meat and drink; but righteousness, and peace, and joy in the Holy Ghost." We also find in Titus 2:13 these words: "Looking for that blessed hope, and the glorious appearing of the great God and our Saviour Jesus Christ…" (KJV).

"Thy will be done in earth, as it is in heaven."

Oftentimes our focus is not on God's will; it's on what we want. But we should pray for His will to be done on the earth just as it is in heaven. Once we come to the conclusion that it's about God's will, then we'll begin to see God move like never before. When we obey God, surrender our lives, situations, and circumstances to the Father, then we'll be able to see Him show up. In Matthew 26:36-39, the Bible says, "Then cometh Jesus with them unto a place called Gethsemane, and saith unto the disciples, Sit ye here, while I go and pray yonder. And he took with him Peter and the two sons of Zebedee, and began to be sorrowful and very heavy. Then saith he unto them, My soul is exceeding sorrowful, even unto death: tarry ye here, and watch with me. And he went a little further, and fell on his face, and prayed, saying O my Father, if it be possible, let this cup pass from me: nevertheless not as I will, but as thou wilt." When we pray for God's will to be done, we are displaying hearts of sincerity and demonstrating trust in God. We need to align ourselves with God's will.

It's a must that we focus on the will of God when we pray, asking Him to perform His will in us and in the earth; asking Him to not only allow us to be hearers of His Word but doers also. Jesus stated in Matthew 7:21, "Not every one that saith unto me, Lord, Lord, shall enter into the kingdom

The Lord's Prayer

of heaven; but he that doeth the will of my Father which is in heaven" (KJV). Also, the Apostle Paul wrote in Romans 12:2, "And be not conformed to this world: but be ye transformed by the renewing of your mind, that ye may prove what is that good, and acceptable, and perfect, will of God" (KJV). As you can see, doing God's will is critically important.

> When we pray for God's will to be done, we are displaying hearts of sincerity and demonstrating trust in God.

In Matthew 18:14, Jesus said, "Even so it is not the will of your Father which is in heaven, that one of these little ones should perish." In the end, God has granted those that are His eternal life through Jesus the Christ. Their portion, their inheritance is the glorious and perfect Kingdom of God, which Christ will establish on the earth in the last days.

God's priorities should become our priorities. We should be more focused on His will than ours, and we should always ask Him to let His will be done on this earth as well as in our lives as individuals.

When praying properly, our focus will be geared towards God's will and not our. We'll not be selfish but will understand that God's will also include His blessings in our lives. It's interesting that Jesus told us God's will is already established in Heaven, but we must ask Him to establish it on the earth. In essence, we must invite God into our earthly affairs. We must also surrender our lives, situations, and circumstances to the Father as Jesus did in the Garden of

Gethsemane when He prayed, "O my Father, if it be possible, let this cup pass from me: nevertheless not as I will, but as thou wilt" (Matthew 26:39).

The next part of the prayer involves us asking God for our spiritual sustenance. Jesus said we must ask the Father,

11 "Give us this day our daily bread."

We know that God is Jehovah-jireh, our provider and our sustainer. Philippians 4:19 says, "But my God shall supply all your need according to his riches in glory by Christ Jesus." We must feed on both natural and spiritual food, which is the Word and revelation of God. Food is a gift from God that enables us to gain strength and keep moving. Just like our bodies need food daily as fuel, our spirits do also. We must feed our spirit man on a daily basis, not just on Sundays.

Next, Jesus teaches us the importance of forgiveness in prayer. He said,

12 "And forgive us our debts, as we forgive our debtors."

We must ask God for His forgiveness on a daily basis. This reminds us that we are not perfect. We need to ask God to forgive us for sins known and unknown. But in the second part of that verse, Jesus told us to forgive others also: "And forgive us our sins; for we also forgive every one that is indebted to us." If we can't forgive others, God can't forgive us. Just like we want and need forgiveness, we need to be forgiving. The Bible tells us in Matthew 18:21-22,

> "Then came Peter to him, and said, Lord, how oft shall my brother sin against me, and I forgive him? Till seven times? Jesus saith unto him, I say not unto thee, Until seven times: but, Until seventy times seven."

Also, in Mark 11:25-26, we find these words:

> "And when ye stand praying, forgive, if ye have ought against any: that your Father also which is in heaven may forgive you your trespasses. But if ye do not forgive, neither will your Father which is in heaven forgive your trespasses."

Jesus told us in Luke 6:37, "Judge not, and ye shall not be judged: condemn not, and ye shall not be condemned: forgive, and ye shall be forgiven." He also said in Luke 17:3-4, "Take heed to yourselves: If thy brother trespass against thee, rebuke him; and if he repents, forgive him. And if he trespasses against thee seven times in a day, and seven times in a day turn again to thee, saying, I repent; thou shalt forgive him."

When it seems like forgiveness is difficult or even impossible to give, we must remember that God forgives us and ask Him for the strength to forgive others. We can't afford at any time to walk in un-forgiveness, seeing how it jeopardizes our walk with God. It doesn't matter what happened. Forgive! Un-forgiveness hinders us not just spiritually, but it negatively affects us mentally, emotionally, and physically. It would be nearly impossible to talk to others about the love and forgiveness of God while you're walking around harboring un-forgiveness in your heart.

Lastly, Jesus told us to state these words:

> 13 "And lead us not into temptation, but deliver us from evil: For thine is the kingdom, and the power, and the glory, forever. Amen."

God does not tempt us with sin and evil; Satan does. The Bible says in 1 Corinthians 10:13, "There hath no temptation taken you but such as is common to man: but God is faithful, who will not suffer you to be tempted above that ye are able; but will with the temptation also make a way to escape, that ye may be able to bear it." Here's further proof that God is not the one tempting us with sin and evil:

> James 1:13 (KJV): "Let no man say when he is tempted, I am tempted of God: for God cannot be tempted with evil, neither tempteth he any man."
> Galatians 5:21 (KJV): "Envyings, murders, drunkenness, revelings, and such like: of the which I tell you before, as I have also told you in time past, that they which do such things shall not inherit the kingdom of God."

The Lord's Prayer

Matthew 6:24 (KJV): "No man can serve two masters: for either he will hate the one, and love the other; or else he will hold to the one, and despise the other. Ye cannot serve God and mammon."

1 Corinthians 10:13 (KJV): "There hath no temptation taken you but such as is common to man: but God is faithful, who will not suffer you to be tempted above that ye are able; but will with the temptation also make a way to escape, that ye may be able to bear it."

John 17:15 (KJV): "I pray not that thou shouldest take them out of the world, but that thou shouldest keep them from the evil."

Revelation 12:9 (KJV): "And the great dragon was cast out, that old serpent, called the Devil, and Satan, which deceiveth the whole world: he was cast out into the earth, and his angels were cast out with him."

> God does not tempt us with sin and evil; Satan does.

Satan is the one tempting us with sin. Satan is known by several names in the Bible: Lucifer, the morning star (Isaiah 14:12); the ruler of the demons (Matthew 12:24); the god of this world (2 Corinthians 4:4); the devil and the accuser (Matthew 4:1).

We must be mindful that although it is not a sin to be tempted, it is a sin to yield to the temptation. And when we begin to give in to temptation, we place ourselves in great danger; for the Bible tells us, "The wages of sin is death, but the gift of God is eternal life through Jesus Christ our Lord" (Romans 6:23).

The devil never stops trying to trick and seduce us. He never gives up in trying to tempt us. Under no circumstance should we let our guards down. Peter told us to be "sober and vigilant" because the devil is always on the prowl, searching for someone he can devour (1 Peter 5:8). When we remain in God; when we remain postured before God in prayer, constantly focusing on Him and His will for our lives, then we'll rest in His power, which is far greater than that of Satan's. Remember: Thine is the Kingdom and the power and the glory…forever! Satan has no power compared to God.

CHAPTER 6
Hindrances To Prayer

THE WORD "HINDER" MEANS "TO MAKE IT DIFFICULT FOR somebody to do something or for something to happen" (Oxford Learner's Dictionaries). According to www.Dictionary.com, it is defined as "to prevent from doing, acting, or happening; to stop." I want to show you some things that can actually hinder (prevent, stop) your prayers from being answered:

1. Unconfessed sins. Isaiah 59:2 says, "But your iniquities have separated you from your God, your sins have hidden his face from you, so that he will not hear." The Bible says in Psalm 66:18, "If I regard wickedness in my heart, the Lord will not hear" (NASB). We must live according to the Spirit and not the flesh. We have to ask God, "What do you want?" instead of thinking only about what we want. Oftentimes the

things we want are not what God wants us to have. We must be in agreement with God's will. Like Jesus prayed, we have to tell God "Not my will but thine will be done." Pray and rest in the Lord because He knows what's best for each and every one of us. We do not want to be separated from God because of our iniquities. This is what the Word of God tells us about iniquity's interference with our prayer life:

> Galatians 5:16-18, "I say then: Walk in the Spirit, and you shall not fulfill the lust of the flesh. For the flesh lusts against the Spirit, and the Spirit against the flesh; and these are contrary to one another so that you do not do the things that you wish. But if you are led by the Spirit, you are not under the law.
> We as Christians should not want to fulfill the lust of the flesh."
> 2 Corinthians 5:17: "Therefore, if any man be in Christ, he is a new creature: old things are passed away; behold, all things are become new."
> 1 John 5:14: "This is the confidence we have in approaching God that if we ask anything according to his will he hears us.
> Luke 22:42: "Yet not my will but yours be done."

2. Un-forgiveness hinders to our prayers. There are so many issues that stem from un-forgiveness. Un-forgiveness creates a root of bitterness, hatred, and resentment. These things grow in our hearts and create strongholds that prevent our

Hindrances To Prayer

prayers from being answered.

> Matthew 18:21-22, "…this is a parable of the unforgiving servant, Peter came to him and said Lord, how oft shall my brother sin against me, and I forgive him? Till seven times? Jesus saith unto him, I say not unto thee, until seven times, but until seventy times seven."

First of all, you must forgive yourself. God is waiting for you to forgive yourself. Also, we must forgive others. Someone may say, "You don't know how they hurt me. You don't know how they broke my heart. I need to be healed right now. You don't understand just how badly I'm suffering as a result of the things they did to me." Well, I'm reminded of the time I taught a class several years ago at this church. I taught on forgiveness. And the Holy Spirit reminded me of how we're always talking about how people have hurt us while forgetting about how many people we've hurt. So, when God said that to me, I was like, "Oh my God." It blew me away. We have to allow the Holy Spirit to do surgery on our hearts because un-forgiveness is like a sickness that can prevent us from getting to where God wants us to be. Normally, the people who've hurt us have gone on about their business while we're still trapped in the hurt and are imprisoned by un-forgiveness. We must let the offense go and choose to forgive quickly not for the other person's sake, but for our own. We must choose to forgive others and walk in the love of God towards them. Yes, we must love others, even those who're seemingly unlovable. 1 John 3:18 says, "My little children let us not love in word, neither in tongue, but in deed and in truth." Also, 1 John 4:7 says, "Beloved, let us love one another: for love is of God and every one that loveth is born of God and knoweth God. He that loveth not, knoweth not God for God is love. Beloved if God so loved us we ought also to love one another."

3. Doubt. Doubt is defined as "to waver in opinion or judgment; to be in uncertainty as to belief respecting anything; to hesitate in belief" (Webster Online Dictionary). Doubt is a big hindrance to prayer as revealed in the Word of God:

> James 1:6: "But let him ask in faith, with no doubting, for the one who doubts is like a wave of the sea that is driven and tossed by the wind" (English Standard Version).
> Matthew 21:21: "And Jesus answered them, 'Truly, I say to you, if you have faith and do not doubt, you will not only do what has been done to the fig tree, but even if you say to this mountain, 'Be taken up and thrown into the sea,' it will happen.'"
> Jude 1:22: "And have mercy on those who doubt" (English Standard Version).
> Matthew 14:31: "Jesus immediately reached out his hand and took hold of him, saying to him, 'O you of little faith, why did you doubt?'"
> Luke 24:38: "And he said to them, 'Why are you

troubled, and why do doubts arise in your hearts?'"

Who were some of the doubters in the Bible? Thomas, one of Jesus' own disciples, doubted the resurrection of Christ until he saw Jesus with his own two eyes as revealed in John 20:24-29. It is here that Jesus told us that blessed is the person who believes God though he or she hasn't physically seen Him. In other words, God is more impressed when we believe in Him and His presence and Word without needing any physical evidence of these things unlike those who choose to believe in Him only after they feel or see something. Don't doubt like Thomas did.

Also, Sarah and Abraham demonstrated their doubt over God's promises and ability to give them a child at a ripe old age when they both laughed at God's promise as found in Genesis 17:17-22 and 18:10-15. It's funny that God got the last laugh by blessing them supernaturally with a son and then having Abraham and Sarah name him Isaac, which means "laughter." When God promises to do something in your life, don't doubt Him.

We Need To Pray

CHAPTER 7
Different Types of Prayers

In the Bible, there are different types of prayers we are instructed by God to pray. Here are a few types of prayers:

Prayer of Agreement

What is the Prayer of Agreement? It is a prayer where two or more people come together with one mind and they begin to petition God, standing on His Word and believing Him for something specific. This prayer is summed up in Matthew 18:19-20 where Jesus said, "Again I say unto you, That if two of you shall agree on earth as touching anything that they shall ask, it shall be done for them of my Father which is in heaven. 20. For where two or three are gathered together in my name, there am I in the midst of them" (Life in the Spirit Study Bible). When we can come together with one accord, agreeing according to the Word of God, we'll begin to experience incredible power and authority in prayer.

I remember once when I had to enter into an agreement in prayer with another individual to believe God for a miracle, one that we needed desperately and quickly. This individual and I came together in the power of agreement, declared the promises of God's Word together, and believe together for God to move in a situation. I firmly believe that this was the reason that individual and I witnessed the hand of God moving in a miraculous way in the midst of that situation.

Here are a few Bible verses that talk to us about the power of agreement in prayer:

> 1 John 3:22: "And whatsoever we ask, we receive of him, because we keep his commandments, and do those things that are pleasing in his sight."
> 1 John 5:14-15: "And this is the confidence that we have in him, that, if we ask anything according to his will, he heareth us: And if we know that he hear us, whatsoever we ask, we know that we have the petitions that we desired of him. If you want your prayers to be effective they must come in agreement and in harmony with God's will if we expect Him to hear and answer us."
> Matthew 6:33: "But seek ye first the kingdom of God,

Different Types of Prayers

and his righteousness and all these things shall be added unto you."

Exodus 17:8-13: "Then came Amalek, and fought with Israel in Rephidim. And Moses said unto Joshua, Choose us out men, and go out, fight with Amalek: tomorrow I will stand on the top of the hill with the rod of God in mine hand. So Joshua did as Moses had said to him, and fought with Amalek: and Moses, Aaron, and Hur went up to the top of the hill. And it came to pass, when Moses held up his hand, that Israel prevailed: and when he let down his hand, Amalek prevailed. But Moses' hands were heavy: and they took a stone, and put it under him, and he sat thereon; and Aaron and Hur stayed up his hands, the one on the one side, and the other on the other side; and his hands were steady until the going down of the sun. And Joshua discomfited Amalek and his people with the edge of the sword."

Prayer of Faith

There is another type of prayer called The Prayer of Faith. What is faith? Hebrews 11:1 tells us, "Faith means being sure of the things we hope for and knowing that something is real even if we do not see it" (New Century Version). The Cambridge English Dictionary defines faith as "trust or confidence in something or someone." This is what the Bible says about the prayer of faith:

James 5:13-15: "Is anyone among you suffering ("pain that is caused by injury, illness, loss, etc.; physical, mental, or emotional pain")? Let him pray. Is anyone cheerful? Let him sing praise. Is anyone among you sick? Let him call for the elders of the church, and let them pray over him, anointing him with oil in the name of the Lord. And the prayer of faith will save the one who is sick, and the Lord will raise him up. And if he has committed sins, he will be forgiven."

Isaiah 43:2: "When you pass through the waters, I will be with you; and through the rivers, they shall not overwhelm you; when you walk through the fire you shall not be burned, and the flame shall not consume you" (English Standard Version).

Even if you are suffering and going through trials and tribulation the word of God tells us to pray. Luke 18:1, which contains the Parable of the Persistent Widow, says,

> "And he spake a parable unto them to this end, that men ought always to pray, and not to faint."

When you pray you cannot be afraid to say it, what ever you are standing in need of say it, but you cannot have doubt in your heart when you pray. You got to believe every promise that God has made you in His word. Numbers 23:19 says God is not a man that He should lie, neither is He the son of man that He should repent; for whatever He said, shall He

Different Types of Prayers

not do it? Or whatever He has spoken, will He not make it good? Romans 4:3 says, "For what saith the scripture? Abraham believed God, and it was counted unto him for righteousness. Believe God and do not doubt because whatever He says it shall come to pass." Not only are we to believe, but we must receive. The Word of God tells us in Matthew 7:7-8, "Ask, and it shall be given you; seek, and ye shall find; knock, and it shall be opened unto you: For every one that asketh receiveth; and he that seeketh findeth; and to him that knocketh it shall be opened." You have to put your faith in action as demonstrated in these two passages of Scripture:

> Matthew 12:13: "Then saith he to the man, Stretch forth thine hand. And he stretched it forth; and it was restored whole, like as the other."
>
> Luke 4:40: "Now when the sun was setting, all they that had any sick with divers diseases brought them unto him; and he laid his hands on every one of them, and healed them."
>
> Hebrews 11:6: "And without faith it is impossible to please Him, for he who comes to God must believe that He is, and He is a rewarder of those who diligently seek Him."

Prayer of Worship

What is worship? It is defined as "to adore; to pay divine honors to; to reverence" according to the KJV Dictionary. In the New Combined Bible Dictionary and Concordance, "worship" means "honor and respect shown to a person." So, worship is the act of reverencing God while thanking Him for all He has done for us. God deserves our worship not simply because of what He has done for us, but because of who He is. Worship first takes place in our hearts before it is expressed outwardly. Worship takes place when we pour out our souls to God and confess before Him that we can do nothing without Him. Here are a couple of verses that talk about worship:

> Psalm 29:2: "Give unto the Lord the glory due unto his name; worship the Lord in the beauty of holiness." Psalm 95:6: "O come, let us worship and bow down: let us kneel before the Lord our maker."

Prayer of Binding and Loosing

The word "bind" means "to tie, or confine with a cord, chain, to fetter, restrain or hold by physical force or influence of any kind" (Webster Revised Unabridged Dictionary). The word "loose" means "to unbound; untied; detach; to set free; to relieve." Jesus said in Matthew 16:19, "I will give you the keys of the kingdom of heaven; whatever you bind on earth will be bound in heaven, and whatever you loose on earth will be loosed in heaven (Life Application Study Bible). In this passage, "keys" represent "full authority." So, not only do we have access to this authority, but we have both the right and an obligation to use it. Jesus gave us this authority in the earth. The word "authority" in Greek is *exousia*, and it means

Different Types of Prayers

"unrestrained right or freedom of action."

INTERCESSORY PRAYER

The word "intercede" means "to plead someone's case" according to the Life Application Study Bible. According to The Free Dictionary, the word "intercede" means "a prayer to God on behalf of another." Basically, intercession is the act of intervening or mediating between differing parties; in particular, it is the act of praying to God on behalf of another person.

In the Bible, Jesus is revealed to be our greatest intercessor. One of the greatest examples of intercession can be found in John chapter 17 where Jesus prays for His disciples and for future Believers. And God is always looking for someone to stand in the gap for others through prayer and intercession. It is stated in Ezekiel 22:30, "And I sought for a man among them, that should make up the hedge, and stand in the gap before me for the land, that I should not destroy it: but I found none." Here are a few more verses on intercession:

> Roman 8:26-27: "In the same way, the Spirit helps us in our weakness. We do not know what we ought to pray for, but the Spirit himself intercedes for us with groans that words cannot express. And he who searches our hearts knows the mind of the Spirit because the Spirit intercedes for the saints in accordance with God's will."

Roman 8:34: "Who is he that condemns? Christ Jesus, who died - more than that, who was raised to life - is at the right hand of God and is also interceding for us."

Hebrew 7:23-25: "Now there have been many of those priests since death prevented them from continuing in office; but because Jesus lives forever, he has a permanent priesthood. Therefore he is able to save completely those who come to God through him because he always lives to intercede for them."

Isaiah 53:10-12: "Yet it was the Lord's will to crush him and cause him to suffer, and though the Lord makes his life a guilt of offering, he will see his offspring and prolong his days, and the will of the Lord will prosper in his hand. After the suffering of his soul, he will see the light of life, and be satisfied, by his knowledge my righteous servant will justify many, and he will bear their iniquities. Therefore I will give him a portion among the great, and he will divide the spoils with the strong, because he poured out his life unto death, and was numbered with the transgressors. For he bore the sin of many, and made intercession for the transgressors."

WHO WERE SOME OF THE MOST EFFECTIVE INTERCESSORS IN THE BIBLE?

1. Abraham: He asked God to spare Sodom in order to save his nephew, Lot. He appealed to the mercy of God and ques-

Different Types of Prayers

tioned whether or not He would slay the righteous with the wicked. Genesis 18:20-20 records: "Then the Lord said, The outcry against Sodom and Gomorrah is so great and their sin so grievous that I will go down and see if what they have done is as bad as the outcry that has reached me. If not, I will know. The men turned away and went toward Sodom, but Abraham remained standing before the Lord. Then Abraham approached him and said: Will you sweep away the righteous with the wicked? What if there are fifty righteous people in the city? Will you really sweep it away and not spare the place for the sake of the fifty righteous people in it?" Sadly, the people of Sodom were too wicked to be spared although Abraham pleaded on their behalves. But God did spare the righteous: He allowed Lot to escape with his family before judging that city.

2. Moses: In Exodus 32:9-14, we find these words: "'I have seen these people,' the Lord said to Moses, 'and they are a stiff-necked people. Now leave me alone so that my anger may burn against them and that I may destroy them. Then I will make you into a great nation.' But Moses sought the favor of the Lord his God. 'O Lord,' he said, 'why should your anger burn against your people, whom you brought out of Egypt with great power and a mighty hand? Why should the Egyptians say, 'It was with evil intent that he brought them out, to kill them in the mountains and to wipe them off the face of the earth? Turn from your fierce anger; relent and do not bring disaster on your people. Remember your

servants Abraham, Isaac, and Israel, to whom you swore by your own self, I will make your descendants as numerous as the stars in the sky and I will your descendants all this land I promised them, and it will be their inheritance forever.' Then the Lord repented, and did not bring on his people he had threatened." Moses, due to his intercession on behalf of the Israelites, caused God to avoid destroying them in His wrath. Intercession can stop disasters from falling on people who're out of alignment with God's Word and will, giving them enough time to repent.

3. In the New Testament, we see Christians interceding on behalf of various individuals. For example, in Acts 12:5, we read: "Peter, therefore, was kept in prison: but prayer was made without ceasing of the church unto God for him." Notice how the New Testament Believers handled persecution; they did so with fervent prayer. James had died and King Herod had placed Peter in the custody under the supervision of sixteen armed guards. Peter knew he was about to be executed by King Herod, and so did the church. But the church understood the power of prayer and intercession, knowing that "the effectual fervent prayer of a righteous man availeth much" (James 5:16), and they refused to stop praying for Peter's deliverance from King Herod's hands. They prayed and prayed and prayed, and God soon answered their prayers.

Here are a few more examples in the Bible:

1 Samuel 7:5: "And Samuel said, Gather all Israel to

Different Types of Prayers

Mizpeh, and I will pray for you unto the Lord."

1 Chronicles 21:17: "And David said unto God, Is it not I that commanded the people to be numbered? Even I it is that have sinned and done evil indeed; but as for these sheep, what have they done? Let thine hand, I pray thee, O Lord my God, be on me, and on my father's house; but not on thy people, that they should be plagued."

2 Chronicles 30:18: "For a multitude of the people, even many of Ephraim, and Manasseh, Issachar, and Zebulun, had not cleansed themselves, yet did they eat the Passover otherwise than it was written. But Hezekiah prayed for them, saying, The good Lord pardon everyone."

We Need To Pray

Spiritual Warfare Prayer

Father God, in the name of Jesus, I come to You as humbly as I can. I realize that we are in a spiritual war; I, therefore, plead the Blood of Jesus over my mind, body, soul, and spirit. The Blood of Jesus is against every demonic force that tries to come against me, my family, and my friends. The Blood of Jesus is against you, Satan, and as God declared over me in His Word, "no weapon formed against thee shall prosper. Every tongue that rises against thee I shall be condemned. This is the heritage of the servants of the Lord, and their righteousness is of me, saith the Lord."

Thank You God that the Blood of Jesus is protecting me from all hurt, harm, and danger. I come against every hindering force, and against every spirit that tries to keep me from praying, studying the Word of God, and walking confidently and courageously in God. I come against every principality, the spiritual wickedness in high places; every spirit of anxiety, depression, suppression, and oppression; against every spirit of sickness, un-forgiveness, and bitterness - I cast you down now in Jesus name.

2 Corinthians 10:4-5 says, "For the weapons of our warfare are not carnal, but mighty through God to the pulling down of strongholds, casting down imaginations, and every high thing that exalteth itself against the knowledge of God, and bringing into captivity every thought to the obedience of Christ." I am covered in the Blood of Jesus, and it is because I am covered under Christ's Blood that Satan cannot and will not get the victory in my life; for I am more than a conqueror through Christ Jesus. If God be for me, then who can stand against me?

I ask You Father in the name of Jesus to destroy any assignments, plans, and works that Satan has designed to hinder and destroy us. It is the anointing that destroys every yoke and bondage of Satan and removes every burden. Father, in the name of Jesus, destroy every bondage over my life and on my family. Lord, we need freedom, we need salvation, and we need healing from all sicknesses, diseases, infirmities, afflictions, hurts, broken-heartedness, and pains. Lord, we need deliverance from un-forgiveness. I am standing on the Word of God found in John 16:23, which says, "And in that day ye shall ask me anything. Verily, verily, I say unto you, Whatsoever ye shall ask the Father in my name, he will give it to you."

I realize that I am in a spiritual war, therefore, God

Spiritual Warfare Prayer

has given me the whole armor of God to put on and has instructed me to be strong in the Lord and in the power of His might. Today, I have on the whole armor of God so that I may be able to stand against the wiles of the devil. Lord, I know we aren't wrestling against flesh and blood but against principalities, against power, against the rulers of the darkness of this world, against spiritual wickedness in high places. I will continue to stand, having my loins girt about with truth, and having on the breastplate of righteousness. With my feet shod with the preparation of the Gospel of peace; and above all, taking the shield of faith, wherewith I shall be able to quench all the fiery darts of the wicked. I will also take the helmet of salvation and the sword of the Spirit, which is the Word of God. I will pray always with all prayer and supplication in the Spirit.

Luke 18:1 says, "Men ought always to pray, and not to faint." I will not faint. I will not give in. I will continue to stand on the Word of God. I will continue in prayer because Romans 12:12 tells us to rejoice in hope, be patient in tribulation, and be instant in prayer. I am rejoicing because God is the hope of glory, and I shall continue to pray because "the effectual fervent prayer of a righteous man availeth much."

I thank You God for strengthening me in this time of spiritual warfare. I am like a tree that is planted by the rivers of waters. I cannot be moved. I have the victory because the greater One lives on the inside of me. I am more than a conqueror through Christ Jesus who strengthens me. Amen.

We Need To Pray

Frequently Asked Questions About Prayer

1. WHY SHOULD WE PRAY?

We should pray mainly for four reasons:

1. God commands us to pray. Philippians 4:6 says, "Be careful for nothing but in everything by prayer and supplication with thanksgiving let your requests be made known unto God." God wants us to come to him in prayer and to bring all of our request and concerns to Him. He loves us and cares about the things we go through. Jesus also said in Luke 18:1, "And he spake a parable unto them to this end, that men should always to pray, and not to faint."
2. Prayer brings us closer to God. James 4:8 says, "Draw

nigh to God, and he will draw nigh to you." To draw near to God means to get as close to Him as possible. How do we get closer to God? By talking to Him and studying His Word. The Apostle Paul wrote in 2 Timothy 2:15, "Study to shew thyself approved unto God, a workman that needeth not to be ashamed, rightly dividing the word of truth." When we draw close to God through prayer, we will begin to experience God's peace. The Apostle Paul wrote in Philippians 4:7, "And the peace of God which passeth all understanding shall keep your hearts and minds through Christ Jesus." Also, when we draw close to God in prayer, we will gain strength. The Bible says in Psalm 29:11, "The Lord will give strength unto his people the Lord will bless his people with peace." Thirdly, when we draw close to God in prayer, we will receive divine guidance. Psalm 40:1-2 says, "I waited patiently for the Lord and he inclined unto me, and heard my cry. He brought me up also out of a horrible pit, out of the miry clay, and set my feet upon a rock, and established my goings."

3. We should pray because God commands us to. We should do it out of obedience to God's command. 1 Samuel 15:22 says, "And Samuel said, Hath the Lord as great delight in burnt offerings and sacrifices, as in obeying the voice of the Lord? Behold to obey is better than sacrifice, and to hearken than the fat of rams." Also, Isaiah 1:19-20 says, "If ye be willing and obedient, ye shall eat the good of the land. But if ye refuse and rebel, ye shall be

devoured with the sword for the mouth of the Lord hath spoken it."
4. We should pray in order to overcome temptation. In Matthew 26:41, Jesus said, "Watch and pray that ye enter not into temptation. The spirit indeed is willing but the flesh is weak." Also, Ephesians 6:18 says, "Praying always with all prayer and supplication in the Spirit and watching thereunto with all perseverance and supplication for all saints."

2. TO WHOM DO WE PRAY?

We pray to the Father in the name of Jesus Christ as the Holy Spirit guides us as explained in Romans 8:26, which reads: "Likewise the Spirit also helpeth our infirmities, for we know not what we should pray for as we ought but the Spirit itself maketh intercession for us with groanings which cannot be uttered. And he that searcheth the hearts knoweth what is the mind of the Spirit because he maketh intercession for the saints according to the will of God."

3. WHAT DOES A.C.T.S. MEAN WHEN WE PRAY?
A-Adoration
C-Confession
T-Thanksgiving
S-Supplication

4. HOW TO DO WARFARE PRAYING?

The name of Jesus is the most powerful name under heaven.

We Need To Pray

There is no name above the name of Jesus. In the name of Jesus Satan will flee and whatever strongholds we may be experiencing must flee also.

God allowed His Son, Jesus, to die on the cross for each and every one of us. It was the Blood of Jesus that became the atonement for our sins. The Blood of Jesus will never lose its power. For the Word of God is quick, and powerful, and sharper than any two-edged sword, piercing even to the dividing asunder of soul and spirit, and of the joints and marrow, and is a discerner of the thoughts and intents of the heart (Hebrews 4:12).

> You should pray in order to overcome temptation.

Jesus is the Word as revealed in John 1:1, which reads: "In the beginning was the Word, and the Word was with God, and the Word was God." Here are a few other verses to consider:

> Matthew 4:4: "But he answered and said, It is written, Man shall not live by bread alone, but by every word that proceedeth out of the mouth of God."
> Isaiah 40:8: "The grass withereth, the flower fadeth: but the word of our God shall stand forever."

More Bible Verses On Prayer

Matthew 6:7: "But when ye pray, use not vain repetitions, as the heathen do: for they think that they shall be heard for their much speaking."

Matthew 7:7: "Ask, and it shall be given you; seek, and ye shall find; knock, and it shall be opened unto you."

Matthew 7:11: "If ye then, being evil, know how to give good gifts unto your children, how much more shall your Father which is in heaven give good things to them that ask him?"

Matthew 21:22: "And all things, whatsoever ye shall ask in prayer, believing, ye shall receive."

We Need To Pray

Mark 11:24: "Therefore I say unto you What things soever ye desire, when ye pray, believe that ye receive them, and ye shall have them."

Luke 18:1: "And he spake a parable unto them to this end, that men ought always to pray, and not to faint."

John 14:13-14: "And whatsoever ye shall ask in my name, that will I do, that the Father may be glorified in the Son. If ye shall ask any thing in my name, I will do it."

Philippians 4:6: "Be careful for nothing; but in every thing by prayer and supplication with thanksgiving let your requests be made known unto God."

1 Thessalonians 5:17: "Pray without ceasing."

1 John 5:14-15: "And this is the confidence that we have in him, that, if we ask any thing according to his will, he heareth us: 15 And if we know that he hear us, whatsoever we ask, we know that we have the petitions that we desired of him."

2 Chronicles 7:14: "If my people, which are called by my name, shall humble themselves, and pray, and seek my face, and turn from their wicked ways; then will I hear from heaven, and will forgive their sin, and will heal their land."

Psalm 4:1: "Hear me when I call, O God of my righteousness, thou hast enlarged me when I was in distress; have mercy upon me, and hear my prayer."

Psalm 145:18: "The Lord is nigh unto all them that call upon him, to all that call upon him in truth."

Proverbs 15:29: "The Lord is far from the wicked, but he heareth the prayer of the righteous."

Notes & References

Chapter One
1. (https://managementmania.com/en/basic-model-of-social-communication)

Chapter Two
1. Godwin, Johnnie; Godwin, Phyllis; Dockery, Karen. *The Student Bible Dictionary Expanded and Updated Edition*. Barbour Books, 2014, p. 216.

Chapter Three
1. Ridolfi, Brian. *What Does The Bible Say About...*, *The Ultimate Answer Book*; AMG Publishers (6815 Shallowford Rd. Chattanooga, Tn. 37421).

Chapter Four
1. *The Concise Bible Dictionary 1997, 2001*. Broadman & Holman Publishers.

Chapter Five
1. Johnson, Barton W. *People's New Testament* (Commentary on Matthew 6:5).

www.ingramcontent.com/pod-product-compliance
Lightning Source LLC
Chambersburg PA
CBHW020429010526
44118CB00010B/495